Inside Out

Kirsten Morgan

Second Place Winner of The Poetry Box Chapbook Prize 2023

Poems © 2024 Kirsten Morgan
All rights reserved.

Editing & Book Design by Shawn Aveningo Sanders
Cover Image licensed via Pixabay
Cover Design by Shawn Aveningo Sanders
Author Photo (p.45) by Greg Hoyle

No part of this book may be republished without permission
from the author, except in the case of brief quotations
embodied in critical essays, epigraphs, reviews and articles,
or publisher/author's marketing collateral.

Second Place Winner of The Poetry Box Chapbook Prize 2023
ISBN: 978-1-956285-50-5
Published in the United States of America.
Wholesale Distribution by Ingram Group

Published by The Poetry Box, February 2024
Portland, Oregon, United Sates
website: ThePoetryBox.com

For women of The Gathering Place—bearers of burdens, tellers of tales, and models of grit, spirit and relentless hope. May you all make your way home.

Author Note

Kirsten was a longtime volunteer at Denver's Stout Street Homeless Clinic and later founded a weekly writing class at The Gathering Place, a women's day shelter. Ten years of close contact with this unique population yielded relationships, insights and hundreds of stories, a few of which are poetically represented in this book. Every woman is real and every story is true, although names and a few identifying details have been altered.

Poems

In the alley	9
Inside Out	10
Street Prayer	11
Why You Must Write	13
Beatrice	14
At a Loss for Words	16
Susanna	17
Rose	18
Ophelias	20
Margaret	21
Cynthia	22
Tina	23
Anything Helps	24
And They Can Only Keen	25
Danielle	26
It's Best Not to Look	27
Gas station bathrooms	28
Grace	29
Medicaid Care Center	30
Kim	31
Hope Springs	33
Skin Deep	34
My Name is Meg	36
Crystal	37
At Your Mercy	38
Vigil	39
Today's Writing Prompt	41

"I just want to feel like a person again."

—Kim Holder, Gathering Place client

In the alley

behind
the homeless clinic

stenciled
on a dumpster

NO BABIES

Inside Out

At the wrong end of Broadway,
where few venture
without bad business,

        mingle the others of our city,
        untidy, fearful, huddled
        masses yearning,
        for anything, everything.

Their eyes look for scraps,
watch for holes,
each person a threat,
each encounter a trial.

    They leave few ripples,
    stay invisible.

    This life is unkind
    to health and can't
    remember ease.

It falls between scaffolds
and holds on for dear life

        as the world looks
        the other way,
        tossing its leftovers

        into alleys and
        under bridges.

Street Prayer

This prayer is for women who carry
their lives in bags and minds in sieves,

who tiptoe through beasts of cities
    where blinders are issued at the gate,
    where breasts speak to hungry men
who trade protection for sex,

    where they wander labyrinths
with snapping streets, stenching alleys
    and no place to sleep
    untouched.

These women once had homes and men
who beat them, then told them they were lucky.
    They had children who can't forgive
    their mothers
    for spreading bread with fear.

This prayer is for that band of nomads
who cling together through the day,
    then scatter

into streets at night, creatures who can see
    through eyelids,
smell threats like coming rain,
    feet bound,
    hands perpetually tied.

Through it all, their Savior stays real and near.
    They talk with Him, whine at Him,
    still trust the only man who seems to care,

but one believer, on a bitch of a mean-ass day,
just couldn't hold back.

[. . .]

"Sweet Jesus," she wailed,
>"I keep prayin' and prayin' and still don't hear
>no answers.
>
>Where are you, Lord, when we need you—
>drinkin' cheap wine and sleepin' it off,
>like all the other men?"

Why You Must Write

This is how you bury the scurry
       beetles of your hurry brain
         those that roll balls   of dung all day

      dig them up   roll them bury them again.

This is how
you rope the wild horses that fury your nights,
      drag your hurry   through dust

      toward the bitter balm of another
      day on the streets.

This is why your pen must dice that grief
      into pieces too tiny
to weigh
          hurry hurry you'll never

get free until you bury them
     in paper   until you

         carve them into creases
sanctified with sweat   laved

in the ink of blood and watch

     each page like a folded boat   float
                        to the sea.

See the water swirl with blood.

See the boats sink.

Feel you float.

Beatrice

I think of you
far too often not to wonder
where you went
when you slid out the door like butter
off a hot pan
I think of how your first words left scars
on sweat-stabbed pages
silent screams
begging
that someone hear someone
too gagged and girded
to speak

I knew this wasn't you
the woman who once put numbers in order
got a paycheck
turned a key and heard the bolt
shift to safety
now the job gone money gone home gone
and your daughter in college free
you followed her here
because she was all you had

I remember the way your sass slipped out
the only true thing in a sty of lies
where help was a theory
and stuck was a way of life
how you spoke it straight
while those who pulled your strings
slunk a crooked path
with muddy mouths and side-shift eyes
I can't forget

as empty months slogged by
those poems you flung onto paper
with a feather

dipped in grease
words like flapping birds
always trying to take flight
I can still see you

holding your ear
to the page and waiting for the next
day to step from behind
your grief and say
it was just kidding
here is a job here is a paycheck here

is a house and a promise
that the world will see the you
behind the laugh and voice
shiny as Sunday song in the church you love

because you will have revised yourself
from this latest of many deaths
and everyone who meets you new
will believe
things have always been as smooth
as your easy smile and creamslick words.

At a Loss for Words

Untethered
unhoused
they find each other on the streets
stay close   but not too
move in shifting circles where trust is slippery
but need is greedy

Who else cares
if they fall-break-disappear-lose themselves?
Who else cares
if they're robbed-raped-starved-ignored by the system?

One woman lost her journal
                        to a thief
her soul in words
her real life gone

The perp seemed to need the secrets
of another   to carry her own
needed to step into other shoes
        click her heels three times
to transport her heart back
                home

Who cares   Who will offer solace for lost words
empty puffs of promise
                        when spoken
specks of possibility
                  when written
fluffs of amnesia
              when gone?

Susanna

First to arrive at writing group
you said little
but grabbed a dictionary
as though it were a treasured trove
from an unknown world
You dove in and didn't raise your head
until you had found
a hidden cache
always three words new to you
carefully copied with definitions
and then you smiled

rebuke   disengagement   plucky

A woman of silence   mussed clothing
ripe aroma   unbrushed teeth   you rose
above the life you hadn't chosen
into the one you could tame

nefarious   estrangement   bombast

The others had been writing for half an hour
when you began your sentences
each with an unearthed word
that lifted you from this bleak day
into a smooth and silken world
.
fastidious   beguiling   innocuous

Rose

I'm not sure
how you stayed upright   so much anger
pinning you down

they took you
from your mother
who stood arms stuck to sides
eyes dry   teeth clamped
as the old Ford chugged away
leaving only dust
behind

Seven years old they took you
to the school
where they would sculpt and polish
a new child
whiteish   shed of heathen ways
the gibberish
of your language   wrongness of your customs

abuse you to disabuse you of memories
stand you cold naked in the bathroom at midnight
for wetting the bed   leave you there
until you stopped sobbing

force strange food in your mouth
until you gagged
thinking you would soon   swallow
their lies
grow strong from their flavors

foreswear your people
forget your tainted skin and vulgar tongue
forget life in the wild   no walls   no plow   no laws
forego the wish to dance   to sing   to praise
the sun and seasons food and family

But you would not
be contained
would not bend to strangeness
so screamed   bit   kicked   flailed all day and through
        each night
until
they threw you in the Ford
drove dusty hours
to the reservation where your   mother had watched
the road for months

dumped you   savage child
hopeless   depraved   irredeemable
possessed by the devil
beyond all hope
of saving
never to know the truth of their Jesus
their knowing
that all things white
were the only things right

and you   sixty years later   homeless
trapped between two worlds
spit their language
to say those times

for only their words can speak their
cruelty
                            your despair

only their words
sharp
as arrow tips

can etch those scars
        onto the stone
        of shattered
        years

Ophelias

They ever repeat mantras
clutched to their breasts
like flowers—

here today,
wilted tomorrow,

this for hope,
this for remembrance
and this one,

feel the thorns,
for promises broken.

We know what we are
but know not what we may be.

Roses for you.
Rue for us.

Margaret

Vulture-hunched,
elbows raised,
this bird of pray
scans the writing group
each week,
calculating her worth
against the others.

Who among them
can snare words,
pour them into this
cavern of longing,
for hers are rough
and bleed a bit
when they rub
against each other.

Please, can someone
offer just a small
surcease of pain,
help her write,
perhaps,
some words of hope
or a few prayers
to an absent God?

Cynthia

Your clothes carefully chosen
from thrift shops
hair coiffed
in the shelter's cracked mirror

I imagined the woman you used to be
determined to stay

in the best parts of the life
you once knew
the life beyond lies and purple
beneath concealer
the life of leisure and terror
of smiles for the public and teeth
replaced without fanfare

because it was worth it
because there were no doors in your house
that opened outward

and so you stayed

until he tried to kill you
and you ran fast in every direction
and still can't stop
glancing over your shoulder

because you know
he'll never stop
looking
for you

Tina

You couldn't have
made yourself
smaller
hunched
head down
even your fingers
tucked into balls
caught no one's eye
showed no wish
to be known
I believe
you believed yourself
invisible
I never knew
whether you heard
voices outside your head
but gradually
you wrote
erased
wrote again
folded your paper
unfolded your paper
wrote again
erased
perhaps two lines
survived
maybe fewer
At the end
you once again pleated
that sheet of ciphers
into an origami
of occlusion
tucked it into your bra
and disappeared

Anything Helps

They bring their broken
bodies, begging
for anything.

Can you find, perhaps,

    my shattered
    pieces
    and glue them

    back together?

Please,
    a small smile,
    a touch, some pills,

    lots of pills,

enough
to face these days
without screaming.

    Failing that,
    might you show me

    the way home?

And They Can Only Keen

I search for their stories around
the edges,

but they store secrets

somewhere between
broken teeth and splintered dreams,

gathered
into bundles,
guarded
by keep-out eyes.

I don't want to pry

but to skim off layers,
find
tenderness beneath.

My mother self wants to hold them
close and scold the gods,
those lazy bastards who ignore
human pain

as they frolic in the clouds, promise
sunbeams and birdsong,

but thunder terror and toss lightning
like paper airplanes,

while the naked run for shelter.

Danielle

Everyone wondered what it meant
when you found that huge piece of brown fabric
at a thrift store,
found a needle and thread
and found a monk's robe within its folds.

You announced
that God had called you to bring the word
and soon
they began to gather around you, drawn in
by the crack in your mind that let in
their light.
They would all be saved.

You tried to preach, searched for wisdom, unsure
of what to do next.
God remained silent and soon you lost your way
wandered off
into the desert, and never
returned.

They wondered for a while whether you had risen
into glory,
but most soon forgot the somewhat monk
who kept tripping
over her robe
and couldn't quite hear
a God who whispered
in riddle and garble.

It's Best Not to Look

Park Avenue, the artery that bleeds
from offices to homes,
passes through muddled masses
pasted like plaque against the brick walls
of the Denver Rescue Mission,
the city's others
awaiting their turn

at the five o'clock table
in exchange for a prayer that Jesus
might bless and take them
from the streets, take them home
to His house, or, with luck,
their own.

They watch to see if drivers
will glance their way,
perhaps think kindly of them,
despairing wretched
refuse from the teeming shores
of other lives. How can those
speeding by, they wonder,

not slam on brakes, empty
wallets out the window, and weep so hard
for the sorrows of their brothers and sisters
that they can't see the road
to glory, stretching out
just for them?

Gas station bathrooms

were the easiest
to sneak into, but
they were always cold
and everything
was dirty—clogged
sinks, filthy toilets,
sticky floors.

I carried supplies
in my backpack,
cleaned
every bathroom
I found
and then slept
on the floor
until the knob
rattled.

It made me feel
like a real person again,
leaving things
clean
like that.

Grace

Eighty years old   you stood
      stick straight
      long white hair

jaw clamped
eyes that saw straight through
mendacity

pride in every word and gesture
for you had been honored
among your people
shaman   holy woman   healer.

You wrote with the grace of a swan
words that skimmed paper
with wandering reveries   but wrote nothing
we could search
to find your other years.

You wouldn't seek help
wouldn't take offers of shelter
      too contained
      too many walls

wouldn't take money
had your own ways they say
sold your only true possession
in the parking lot behind the Shell station

in the backseats of cars after dark
      a piece of your holy body
      for enough money to live

like a wild thing

      spend nights in a sleeping bag
      in the alley behind the shelter where no one

      could make you breathe their inside air.

Medicaid Care Center

Each time
I go to visit,
she tells me
she's blessed,

a castaway,
who lives
among the rescued.

They huddle
together
in an old brick building
at the end
of the road,
bound,
muzzled,
ignored.

Urine is their
cold cologne,
they sleep
in stink,
live for bingo
wait to be fed,
wait to die.

She says it again
and I can tell
she means it.
Blessed.

Kim

I loved the way
you spun stories of your travels
thirty years   hundreds of miles

on foot
park benches   ditch toilets
dumpster food   wonders everywhere

      I wasn't always mad you told me
      college job marriage son
      I wasn't always like this

      My whole family had uneasy brains
      and one by one went mad
      my brother jumped off

      a ship at sea
      my mother leapt in
      and out of madness

      every day of her life before she took it
      so when I went mad I wasn't surprised
      couldn't keep a job couldn't keep

      my son dropped him off
      at his father's and now
      he's grown and could be mad too

You loved that word: mad
something about its old-fashioned literary sound
like the aunt in the attic

appealed to your delight in language
your brain diamond dense
and sharp as a scream

[. . .]

loved the dance of words
collected them in haystacks hoping to find
a prick of sanity

We talked for hours about the world
about politics
religion the ways humans

seek safety
about visits each night
from Archangel Gabriel

who instructed you in ways of the spheres
who pulled you through the veil
then pushed you

back again before the sun
who told you who had died
in the night and who

would leave soon and you didn't tell me
but I think he named you next
because you said good-bye in a different way

when I left that last time
and when I came to visit again
you had tossed your bonds

to pace upon the mountains overhead
and hide your face
*amid a crowd of stars**

---

* after William Butler Yeats

Hope Springs

These vessels,
victims of slings and arrows,
hold their outrageous fortunes
welded into armor,

while their tender places stay swaddled in silk,
a sleight of cobbled memories
and bleached wishes.

When lights dim,
they pull out the best of other times
and study them like maps to somewhere else,
relentless believers
that only a stroke of fortune lies between
now and wonders to come,

new life waiting for a roll of dice,
winning numbers,
perhaps a bag of gold

dropped carelessly on the street.

Skin Deep

"Merry Christmas," he said,
then pointed the shotgun at her head,
pulled the trigger and watched
her fall to the floor, dead.

"Heard a shot," he told the police.
"Found her in the alley.
Dragged her in.
Never seen her before."

She didn't die, but lay
in the hospital, a Jane Doe,
not quite alive, not quite dead.
It took her sister three days
to track her down.

She lived, but Medicaid
just covered damages.
With half a face, skin grafted
over nothing,
she hid from the world.

A year later, Oprah heard,
filmed her, face blurred,
and asked the country for help.

Money flowed, plastic surgeries
sculpted missing parts—
new skin, new jaw, new cheek,
new nose, new eye, new teeth,
something from nothing.

"I'm here to write a book,"
she told the writing group.
a new woman with a whole face,
beautiful, almost
symmetrical, almost smooth.
"He was my boyfriend for 26 years.
When he gets out of prison,
we're gonna get married."

My Name Is Meg

She shuffled into the writing group
with bowed head
and rounded back, afraid
to be there, needing to be there,

sat quietly, pen over paper,
but couldn't

connect
thoughts to words.

Weeks passed,
and then a cramped sentence.

Finally,
two sentences.
Then three.

On the day I broke
her words into lines
and made them a poem,
she smiled and asked
how to do it.

Then she wrote
in a flurry, storms
of words that couldn't stop.

A few months later,
when a guest came to visit,
the writers told their names.
She looked him in the eye
and declared
with a shy smile,

My name is Meg,
and I'm a poet.

CRYSTAL

You sashay into the writing room,
        butt-swinging,
smile-slinging happy—
        dress too tight, pearls chipped,
unaccustomed high-heel elegance.

Got me an interview—
        gonna get a job and leave
        the street forever.
I feel soooo sweet!

You flounce like a runway model,
        back and forth, holding tightly
to slippage—circle, pose,
        wait for compliments.

And of course they come—
        whistles, shrieks,
        woo-wee, you go girl,
others seeing themselves traveling
        in style one day.

You're restless, try on words
for a while, then revert
        to your body's other language,
        pull out old tricks,
affects, postures—
        imagine, remember, hope.

        I look sooo good!
How could anyone turn me down?"

At Your Mercy

We are faceless, homeless,
silent, invisible
as we collect your alms each year.

We are ashamed and proud, terrified
and hopeful, grieving yet grateful
for bits of your safety.

We are wanderers, ramblers,
nomads, pilgrims searching,
for solid ground and full bellies.

We're philosophers, soul-searchers,
mystics, truth-tellers who lie
to survive falsehoods.

We are scapegraces, stigmas, stains
on the veneer of your perfect world,
and we do not exist

unless you choose to see us.

Vigil

On a blue-cold evening each December,
we gather outside
the City and County Building,
all born-free-equal-under-the-law people who care

that hundreds in the crowd
will sleep outside this night in Denver,

and some will die.

We gather with candles and words,
sing songs of sorrow and say
good-bye to all

who have slipped this coil
in the last twelve months,
speak the names that are known,
those who died
as they lived,
empty of spirit, bereft of bed.

Mary Martinez.   We will remember.
John Jones.   We will remember.

The man in a wheelchair at the corner
of Speer and Broadway.
The woman too sick to leave her cardboard nest
below the overpass. Will we remember?

Most of us go home to warmth,
write a check, dream of sleeping on an iceberg,
feel a knot of hunger
in full stomachs, and by morning

move back into our easy lives,
uneasy in knowing
that some of those who hold a candle tonight

[. . .]

will soon die on a park bench,
in an alley, at the hands
of a thief, a freeze, or exhaustion
from pushing that rock up a mountain.

Today's Writing Prompt

What would you do
if you knew
you could not fail?

The woman without
a bed, who writes
with probity and wades
through mystery,

who is grateful beyond measure
and hopeful without reason,

often hungry.
always in pain,
rarely with a bed,

thinks for only a moment
before writing
in her careful hand,

I would achieve enlightenment.

Early Praise

"I admire how fearlessly these poems bear witness to those who have lived lives most of us cannot fathom, and in this they are attempts to beatify—to make sacred—these women. The poems break and mend my heart for a multitude of reasons, but mostly via the small details and images ('backseats of cars after dark,' 'poems…flung onto paper'). In this way, the book is a collection of odes, powerful expressions of love and compassion."

—Michael Henry, Executive Director, Lighthouse Writers Workshop

"In *Inside Out*, Kirsten Morgan engages with a practice of accompaniment—that is, she walks alongside vulnerable and unhoused women for whom 'help was a theory / and stuck a way of life.' Listening not just to speakers' narratives but to each woman's distinct language of survival, Morgan searches 'for their stories around / the edges.' In so doing, she finds 'wonders everywhere.' This is poetry of witness, always rich with humor and imagination. Many poets do not realize that imagination is a necessary element of empathy. *Inside Out* conveys an empathy that transforms sorrow to resilience."

—Elizabeth Robinson, author of *Excursive* and *Thirst & Surfeit*, winner of a 2022 Pushcart Prize

"A powerful work of empathic imagination. In these searing poems of witness and service, Kirsten Morgan gives voice to the voiceless and takes us into a world most would prefer not to see."

—John Brehm, author of *Dharma Talk* and *No Day at the Beach*

"*Inside Out* is an astounding poetry collection—a startling, superb account of women who've experienced homelessness, addiction, domestic violence and other indignities. 'This life is unkind,' one poem suggests, 'to health and can't / remember ease.' Told about those who struggle daily on the 'snapping streets,' the book never devolves into trite predictability; never sacrifices poetic craft for mere self-expression. These women experience harsh lives, honed sharp by raw pain. Yet their difficult stories never outweigh their deepest truth: they are truth-tellers who've rightfully earned their seat at the literary table."

—Joy Roulier Sawyer, author of *Lifeguards*

About the Author

Kirsten Morgan has taught poetry to children in an independent school, elders in a lifelong learning program, and clients of The Gathering Place, a day shelter for homeless and impoverished women. She is a longtime member of Denver's Lighthouse Writers Workshop, has published many poems in literary journals and was a finalist for The Birdy Prize from Meadowlark Press. She is the author of *Without Skipping a Beat: A Child's Heart Transplant Journey,* editor of *One Day, One Night at a Time: Women Write of Poverty, Homelessness and Hope,* and co-editor of *An Uncertain Age: Poems by Bold Women of a Certain Age.* Kirsten hikes, snowshoes, reads incessantly and writes prose and poetry delightedly, in Denver and snuggled into her house deep in the mountains.